Our Gift to the Beach

Margarita González-Jensen
Photographs by Richard Hutchings

Y0-DAC-032

Rigby • Saxon • Steck-Vaughn

www.HarcourtAchieve.com
1.800.531.5015

Mom and I went
to the beach.

We looked at the beach.
The beach was messy.

We wanted to help the beach.

We picked up cans.
We picked up paper.

We picked up cups.
We picked up bags, too.

8

The beach was clean.
Mom and I were happy.

I found pretty shells.

I picked up the shells.

I found wood.

I picked up the wood.

I found rocks, too.
I picked up the rocks.

I helped the beach,
and I had fun!